Men-at-Arms · 61

The Portuguese Army of the Napoleonic Wars

Otto von Pivka · Illustrated by Michael Roffe
Series editor Martin Windrow

Published in 1977 by
Osprey Publishing, Midland House, West Way, Botley, Oxford
OX2 0PH, UK
443 Park Avenue South, New York, NY 10016, USA
Email: info@ospreypublishing.com

© Copyright 1977 Osprey Publishing Ltd.
Reprinted 2002, 2005

This book is copyrighted under the Berne
Convention. All rights reserved. Apart from any
fair dealing for the purpose of private study,
research, criticism or review, as permitted under
the Copyright Act, 1956, no part of this publication
may be reproduced, stored in a retrieval system, or
transmitted in any form or by any means electronic,
electrical, chemical, mechanical, optical, photo-
copying, recording or otherwise, without the prior
permission of the copyright owner. Enquiries should
be addressed to the Publishers.

CIP Data for this publication is available from the British Library

ISBN 0 85045 251 1
Filmset by BAS Printers Limited, Wallop, Hampshire
Printed in China through World Print Ltd.

Series Editor: MARTIN WINDROW

FOR A CATALOGUE OF ALL BOOKS PUBLISHED BY OSPREY MILITARY AND
AVIATION PLEASE CONTACT:

NORTH AMERICA
Osprey Direct, 2427 Bond Street,
University Park, IL 60466, USA
E-mail: info@ospreydirectusa.com

ALL OTHER REGIONS
Osprey Direct UK, P.O. Box 140, Wellingborough,
Northants, NN8 2FA, UK
E-mail: info@ospreydirect.co.uk

www.ospreypublishing.com

The Portuguese Army of the Napoleonic Wars

Chronology

PORTUGAL'S PART IN THE PENINSULAR WAR, 1806–1813

1806 Nov. Napoleon issues his Berlin Decrees, closing every port on the coastline of Continental Europe to British trade, in an attempt to achieve by blockade what he failed to achieve by naval action. Apart from Sweden the only nation likely to jib at these demands is Portugal. During 1806 and 1807 Napoleon's demands on the House of Bragança increase; it is clear that only complete domination will satisfy him ultimately. Simultaneously he works to increase his grip on the ailing Spanish monarchy.

1807 Oct.–Nov. Junot leads a French army of 30,000 men through Spain – with Spanish agreement – to invade Portugal. Although much weakened by winter forced marches they take Lisbon in November without a fight. Portuguese leaders, including the Prince Regent, take ship for their Brazilian possessions leaving the nation without a focus for resistance, although the will is there.

1808 Early A token Spanish force assists Junot in the occupation of Portugal. The weak army is half disbanded, half absorbed into Napoleon's forces. In May the Portuguese Legion is formed at Grenoble, under the Marquis of Alorna, comprising five regiments of foot and two of horse with a small artillery unit. In the same month Spain finally rises against the thinly disguised occupation by French troops.

1808 May–July One of the Spanish divisions in Junot's army defects, and the other has to be

Police guard of Lisbon (left) and armed peasant – from W. Bradford's *Sketches of Military Costume in Spain and Portugal*, 1814. The guard wears an army pattern shako with black plume; yellow cords, front plate and peak (the latter surely an error!) and yellow chin-strap. The royal blue coat has red facings edged yellow, the blue trousers a yellow stripe. In addition to an infantry musket he carries two pistols in a buff holster and a sabre in a black scabbard on a buff waist-belt. Considering that his musket is cocked, he shows admirable *sang froid* in leaning on its muzzle! The armed peasant of the Algarve wears brown coat and trousers trimmed dark green, gaiters of the same colours, light blue stockings, white buttons, white belts, and a grey greatcoat roll. His black hat has dark green trim and tuft and a red cockade held by a white button

Officer of Engineers and officer of 16th Infantry Regiment, from Bradford's *Sketches*. Bradford shows almost all his figures with the singular blue-within-red cockade just visible at the base of the left-hand officer's plume. A colour treatment of the engineer officer will be found on Plate C; note the eagle-head sabre hilt, with a chain from beak to crossguard. The infantry officer has gold cords, shako plates, lace and and buttons. His dark blue coat has red cuffs and collar, and white turnbacks and front piping. His belt is white, with a silver plate with a raised gold device; his sash is red with silver fringes. This broad frontal piping on the coats of Bradford's subjects, in divisional colour, is absent from other sources such as Dighton, who show conventional narrow piping

disarmed. Communications with French authorities in Spain are cut. In June there are risings in the Algarve and the Oporto region. By late June the French army is concentrated in a defensive perimeter linking Almeida, Elvas, Peniche, Setubal and Lisbon. By mid-July the army is further confined in the area Abrantes–Lisbon–Peniche–Setubal, but continues to mount flying columns to subdue patriots in the surrounding countryside. In late July one such force crushes resistance at Evora with great brutality.

1808 23 July The surrender of General Dupont's army of 17,600 to Andalusian forces at BAYLEN lends new heart to the Spanish insurrection. The French puppet king of Spain, Joseph Bonaparte, panics prematurely and withdraws all French forces north of the Ebro.

1808 1 August British troops commanded by *Sir Arthur Wellesley* land at Mondego Bay in Portugal. After negotiations some 1,600 Portuguese patriot troops join his force – others are offered, but he is unable to provision them from the limited logistic resources at his command.

1808 17 Aug. Anglo–Portuguese force drives in weak French blocking force under Delaborde at ROLICA and continues to advance south.

1808 21 Aug. Wellesley's army, in position at VIMIERO to cover landing of reinforcements in the mouth of the Maceiro river, wins a defensive victory over Junot's army, which it outnumbers by approximately 18,650 to 13,000 men. The 2,000 Portuguese troops present are not engaged, however.

1808 Sept. The Convention of Sintra is concluded by Wellesley's superior, Sir Hew Dalrymple; under its terms Junot is evacuated in British ships, taking his arms and booty. This pact enrages the British people and their politicians and Wellesley, Dalrymple and Sir Harry Burrard are recalled. Wellesley is later exonerated but in the meantime Sir John Moore takes over British forces in the Peninsula.

1808 Sept.–1809 Jan. Moore is ordered to advance into Spain to cooperate with Spanish armies; but the lack of effective liaison and the progressive defeat of Spanish forces by the French leave him isolated. He is forced to continue a hopeless campaign by political pressure; but after a victory over French cavalry in a skirmish at Sahagun on 21 December Moore learns that greatly superior French forces – including a column led by Napoleon in person – are converging on him and is forced to break for the coast at Corunna. The army disintegrates under the gruelling conditions; it partly redeems itself by its defensive victory at CORUNNA on 16 January 1809, to cover its own embarkation. Moore is killed in action.

1809 Mar. Portugal requests aid in reorganizing her forces, and *William Carr Beresford* sails from Britain to take up this task, with the local rank of marshal. (He is recommended by Wellesley, who was first offered the post but declined it.) Wellesley is requested to report to the government on the chances of defending Portugal against the inevitable French re-invasion and states that he is confident of success if given 20,000 men, authority over the Portuguese army, and the continuing distraction of Spanish patriot resistance.

1809 22 Apr. Wellesley returns to Portugal as commander-in-chief, charged with defending the country. Reinforcements bring British forces up to approximately 30,000. By the time he arrives Soult has occupied the northern half of the country down to Oporto, but has advanced no farther south.

1809 May Wellesley sends Beresford northeast to block Soult's possible retreat eastwards, with 4,200 Portuguese and 1,800 British troops. He himself leaves Coimbra on the 8th, with 16,000 British and 2,400 Portuguese, and strikes due north for Oporto. On the 12th he crosses the Duero and drives Soult from OPORTO; the French retreat to the border, which they cross on the 18th.

> Portuguese units involved are: 2nd Bn./16th Line Infantry (Sontag's Brigade); 1st Bn./10th Line Infantry (Alexander Campbell's Brigade); 1st Bn./16th Line Infantry (Stewart's Brigade); and 2nd Bn./10th Line Infantry (Cameron's Brigade).

1809 July Wellesley strikes eastwards into Spain against Victor, in concert with the Spanish general Cuesta's 35,000-strong army. He is hampered by the incompetence of Cuesta and the inexperience of the Spanish troops, but on 27–28 he defeats Victor and Sebastiani (under command of King Joseph and Jourdan) at TALAVERA DE LA REINA. The victory is costly – 5,365 Allied casualties – and manoeuvres by enemy forces threatening his line of retreat force Wellesley to pull back into Portugal, reaching the frontier on 3 September. (There were no Portuguese troops at Talavera, although the Loyal Lusitanian Legion scouted on the flank of the advance and distinguished itself during the retreat.)

1809 Late The Allied field army remains in Portugal, and Wellesley – now Viscount Wellington – busies himself with the preparation of the LINES OF TORRES VEDRAS and the training and organization of the local forces. The Lines are a vast system of linked redoubts guarding the Lisbon peninsula in depth, largely garrisoned by Portuguese militia regiments. The French continue vigorous operations in many parts of Spain, winning spectacular victories.

1810 Apr.–Aug. Masséna leads the new French Army of Portugal in a renewed invasion via the northern corridor. Ciudad Rodrigo, the Spanish border fortress, is besieged on 26 April and falls on 10 July. Craufurd's Light Division, including the 1st and 3rd Portuguese Caçadores, manoeuvres brilliantly before the enemy's advance; but the premature loss of Almeida on 28 August forces Wellington to fall back. This is a planned withdrawal along prepared lines. With 32,000 men he lures Masséna's 65,000 south-west to a strong blocking position at Bussaco, prepared months in advance. There he links up with detached corps under Hill and Beresford, and with a combined army of some 26,000 British and 25,850 Portuguese he awaits Masséna's attack.

1810 27 Sept. Wellington inflicts a severe defeat on Masséna at BUSSACO. The Portuguese army distinguishes itself in its first major battle against the French, vindicating Beresford's forthright methods of reform and the British training cadres, as well as the essential quality of the Portuguese foot soldier.

> Units involved are: 2nd, 4th, 10th and 14th Line Infantry (Hamilton's Division); 9th and 21st Line Infantry (Champlemond's Brigade, Picton's Division); 11th and 23rd Line Infantry (Collins's Brigade, Cole's Division); 3rd and 15th Line Infantry, Tomar Militia (Spry's Brigade, Leith's Division); Loyal Lusitanian Legion, 8th Line Infantry (Eben's Brigade, Leith's Division); 1st and 3rd Caçadores (Light Division); 1st and 16th Line Infantry, 4th Caçadores (Pack's Independent Brigade); 6th and 18th Line Infantry, 6th Caçadores (Campbell's Independent Brigade); 7th and 19th Line, 2nd Caçadores (Coleman's Independent Brigade).

1810 Sept.–1811 Mar. Wellington pulls back into the Lines of Torres Vedras, which are a complete surprise to the French. Guarded by the triple line of redoubts, and with an efficient network of internal communications, the Allies sit out the winter in comfort. All available food and useful materials, and a large part of the civilian population, have been brought into the Lines, and Masséna's army suffers terribly from hunger and exposure as well as from harrassment by Portuguese irregulars. In February Soult's threat to Badajos in the south forces Wellington to detach Beresford with some British and Portuguese units. In March the stalemate is broken. On the 5th Masséna begins his retreat towards Spain, and Wellington follows him; no general action takes place. On the same day, far to the south, Sir Thomas

Officer of the 1st or Alcantara Cavalry Regiment; see Plate B. The white facings and piping refer to the regiment's position in the First or Centre Division of the army. The bit in this sketch was obviously drawn by an equestrian novice!

Graham wins a small but hard-fought battle at Chiclana–Barossa while operating out of Cadiz against Soult's rear; flank companies of the 20th Portuguese Line Infantry take part. This victory cancels out Soult's success at Badajos six days later, when the Spanish garrison treacherously surrender the fortress. Wellington detaches more troops to guard this sector.

1811 Apr.–May Masséna, partially re-provisioned, returns to the offensive and threatens the northern sector in an attempt to relieve his garrison in Almeida. His 48,500 men are faced by Wellington's 37,500 at FUENTES DE ONORO on 3 May.

There is heavy fighting on that day, and a lull between the armies on the 4th. On the 5th Masséna makes a very able attack on the Allied right wing and drives it in, but by the end of the day is still in no position to advance on Almeida. Allied casualties are some 1,804 and French some 2,844; of these totals, about 800 and 1,300 respectively are suffered in savage street-fighting in Fuentas village, where the 3rd Caçadores distinguish themselves. Meanwhile in the south Soult advances with approximately 25,000 men to relieve the garrison of Badajos. Beresford faces him at ALBUERA on 16 May with some 20,000 Anglo-Portuguese and 12,000 Spanish troops. The position is held at the cost of frightful slaughter, two British brigades being virtually wiped out. Both Masséna and Soult withdraw.

Portuguese units involved in the twin battles of May 1811 are:

Fuentes de Onoro: 9th and 21st Line Infantry (Power's Brigade, Picton's Division); 3rd and 15th Line Infantry, 8th Caçadores (Spry's Brigade, Erskine's Division); 8th and 12th Line Infantry (Madden's Brigade, A. Campbell's Division); 7th and 19th Line Infantry, 2nd Caçadores (Doyle's Brigade, Houston's Division); 1st and 3rd Caçadores (Light Division); 6th and 18th Line Infantry, 6th Caçadores (Ashworth's Independent Brigade); 4th and 10th Line Cavalry (Barbaçena's Brigade).

Albuera: 11th and 23rd Line Infantry, one bn. Loyal Lusitanian Legion (Harvey's Brigade, Cole's Division); 2nd, 4th, 10th and 14th Line Infantry (Hamilton's Division); 5th Line Infantry, 5th Caçadores (Collins's Independent Brigade); 1st and 7th Line Cavalry, one sqdn. each 5th and 8th Line Cavalry (Otway's Brigade).

1811 Late Wellington's attempts to take Ciudad Rodrigo and Badajos are foiled by shortage of siege equipment and by threatening moves by two large French combined armies. There are no general engagements, although many skirmishes and outpost actions.

1812 Jan. Withdrawal of French troops for the Russian campaign, and a period of disarray

Novion or Lisbon Police Cavalry, 1809. Different copies of Bradford's book sometimes include contradictory colours: this plate is shown with a black comb and plume on the helmet in one case, but with yellow and red respectively in another! The dark blue coat has red collar and cuffs and – in one copy – a red-within-yellow stripe down the front under the yellow buttons. Lace is yellow, the bandolier red-within-yellow, the buckle-plate yellow. The waistbelt is buff with a yellow plate; the sword has a white grip and a black and yellow scabbard; the white breeches tuck into what appear to be cuffed boots with silver buckle-on spurs. Holster covers are black bearskin, harness black with white metal fittings

in the enemy command structure offer Wellington an opportunity to take the vital frontier fortresses at last. On the 8th the Allies appear before CIUDAD RODRIGO, and on the night of the 19th the fortress is stormed and captured; General Craufurd is among the Allied casualties. Portuguese units of Picton's and Craufurd's divisions, and of Pack's Brigade, distinguish themselves.

1812 Mar.–Apr. Reinforced by a strong artillery train and with some 26,000 Anglo–Portuguese troops, Wellington invests BADAJOS, covered to the south and north-east by detached forces under Graham and Hill numbering some 19,000 and 14,000 respectively. The fortress, much stronger than Ciudad Rodrigo and held by an excellent French garrison of some 4,700, finally falls on 6 April, but at a cost of some 2,200 casualties. The maddened assault troops sack the town with medieval ferocity. Portuguese units committed lose some 400 men.

1812 June Wellington advances eastwards into central Spain with some 28,000 British, 17,000 Portuguese and 3,000 Spanish troops. His adversary is Marmont's Army of Portugal, 52,000 strong. On the 17th Wellington occupies Salamanca.

1812 22 July After a month of complicated manoeuvring for advantage, the armies clash at SALAMANCA. Wellington wins a brilliant victory by seizing a momentary chance to cut Marmont's army in two and defeat it in detail. French losses are 14,000, Allied losses about 5,200.

Portuguese units involved are: 9th and 21st Line Infantry, 12th Caçadores (Powers's Brigade, Pakenham's Division); 11th and 23rd Line Infantry, 7th Caçadores (Stubb's Brigade, Cole's Division); 3rd and 15th

Line Infantry, 8th Caçadores (Spry's Brigade, Leith's Division); 8th and 12th Line Infantry, 9th Caçadores (Rezende's Brigade, Clinton's Division); 7th and 19th Line Infantry, 2nd Caçadores (Collins's Brigade, Hope's Division); 1st and 3rd Caçadores (Light Division); 1st and 16th Line Infantry, 4th Caçadores (Pack's Independent Brigade); 13th and 14th Line Infantry, 5th Caçadores (Bradford's Independent Brigade); 1st and 11th Portuguese Line Cavalry (D'Urban's Brigade)

1812 Late The French abandon much of Spain, although remaining strong in the east and north. Wellington advances north-eastwards and besieges BURGOS without success. The French threaten his rear, and he is forced to withdraw to Portugal once again. The enemy reoccupy much of the ground they had lost, but south of the Tajo the Peninsula remains free, and even in occupied areas the almost unchecked operations of the guerrilleros render the French grip weak and uncertain.

1813 May Planting evidence to suggest that he is planning to march into central Spain once more, Wellington in fact strikes northwards with nearly 60,000 men. A combination of speed, audacious advances through country considered impassable, and brilliant logistic preparation enable him to outflank on the west several successive French lines of defence. The French armies are unable to concentrate for more than a few days on any planned defensive line, before the threat to their right wing forces them to pull back yet again. At last the combined Armies of the South, Centre and Portugal are concentrated, with a strength of some 66,000 men.

1813 21 June With 78,000 men, Wellington wins a decisive victory of envelopment at VITTORIA in the presence of King Joseph. French losses are some 8,000 to 5,100 Allies, but all their artillery and wheeled transport is captured together with a vast treasure. The Allies' looting of this hoard delays their pursuit of the enemy, but by the second week in July the only French troops still under arms in western Spain are the garrisons of San Sebastian and Pamplona.

Portuguese units involved at Vittoria are as follows: 6th and 18th Line Infantry, 6th Caçadores (Ashworth's Brigade, Stewart's Division); 9th and 21st Line Infantry, 11th Caçadores (Powers's Brigade, Picton's Division); 11th and 23rd Line Infantry, 7th Caçadores (Stubb's Brigade, Cole's Division); 3rd and 15th Line Infantry, 8th Caçadores (Spry's Brigade, Oswald's Division); 7th and 19th Line Infantry, 2nd Caçadores (Le Cor's Brigade, Dalhousie's Division); 17th Line Infantry, 1st and 3rd Caçadores (Light Division); 1st and 16th Line Infantry, 4th Caçadores (Pack's Independent Brigade); 13th and 24th Line Infantry, 5th Caçadores (Bradford's Independent Brigade); 2nd, 4th, 10th and 14th Line Infantry, 10th Caçadores (Silveira's Division); 1st, 11th, and 12th Line Cavalry (D'Urban's Brigade); 6th Line Cavalry (Campbell's Brigade).

A FRENCH ASSESSMENT

The Portuguese army of 1807 was not at the peak of military efficiency. As was the case with the neighbouring army of Spain, this was largely due to the decadent state of Portuguese society at that time. The disease had its roots close to the throne of the country, and spread its paralysing tentacles into all corners of state administration and private enterprise.

The usual source quoted on this subject is Charles Oman's passage in his *History of the Peninsular War*. While Oman is a magnificent mine of information, and to be highly recommended as much for his lucid and readable prose as for the depth of his research, the present writer has preferred in this case to quote extensively from the writings of a French authority of the day, who offers the English reader a novel view of the Portuguese army as seen by its enemies, rather than the more usual perspective of its exasperated but patient allies. General Count Maximilian Sebastian Foy was a notably able French brigade and divisional commander during the Peninsular War and the 1815 campaign, and his judgement

Officer, Legion d'Alorna. This experimental formation was raised in Portugal prior to the French invasion of 1808; it consisted of light troops, and the style of this officer's uniform is unmistakably *à la hussard*. See Plate E for colour details

may be accepted as professional and objective. In his *History of the War in the Peninsula*, published in London in 1827, he gives a clear picture of the Portuguese army and the society of which it was a part. The slightly archaic language adds period atmosphere to the passage:

'... Under the direction of Luiz Pinto, Secretary of State, and particularly from 1797 to 1801, the war department manifested an activity to which it had been unaccustomed ever since the campaign of 1762. Several useful regulations for the recruiting and organization of the army were framed or renewed and efforts made to complete it. The period of service of the soldiers of all arms was fixed at ten years. Every year the *captain mor* caused

11

The Portuguese army was naturally obliged to co-operate with the Spanish forces during their joint struggle against the French, particularly along Portugal's long and vulnerable border. These Bradford sketches illustrate a Catalonian Light Infantryman and an artilleryman. The former, a soldier of the division which served on the Baltic with La Romana in 1808, wears a black-crested leather helmet with red cockade and plume and yellow fittings; his green jacket is faced red and laced yellow. Note the characteristic ammunition pouch on the front of the waist-belt. The gaiters have red top trim and tassel. The artilleryman wears the dark blue coat with red facings which was almost a universal uniform for this branch. Lace, buttons and hat trim are yellow, and the plume and sabre-knot are red

a list of the males capable of bearing arms to be drawn up in his district by the captains of *ordenances*, from reviews held on the spot. In concert with the civil authority, he afterwards struck out the privileged persons, the married men, such as had attained the age of thirty-five years, the eldest sons of widows, and those who were particularly serviceable to agriculture and the arts. From the list thus reduced, the contingent required from the captainship for the service of the army of the line was drawn by lot. Very frequently the recruits on whom the lot fell were detained in prison till they were numerous enough to form a marching detachment and to join the regiment. The militia was afterwards recruited in the same manner, but for life. It took bachelors before married men, and did not even spare retired soldiers when they were still able-bodied. The rest of the persons entered in the lists, after the levies for the line and the militia, composed the corps of *ordenances*.

'The officers of the infantry, cavalry, and artillery, were chosen, two-thirds from among the cadets, and one-third from among the sergeants. The cadets are young men who accompany the regiments to learn the profession. The nobles alone could be cadets. Those from the provinces, and especially the poorest, flocked to the army. Above the rank of sub-lieutenant (*afferez*), promotion was not governed by any rule. The college of nobles, one of Pombal's institutions, and the royal academy of fortification, founded by Queen Mary, furnished the army with some distinguished officers: there were also young men of high birth at the head of the regiments and the companies, especially in the cavalry: but the officers in general were ill paid, held in low estimation, and formed a subaltern class in regard to education, and mode of life. From their perpetual sojourn in the same garrisons resulted an indolent life, low habits, and many unequal matches, which extinguished the generous sentiments peculiar to the military profession. For fear the time should ever return when officers waited at the tables of the Fidal-goes, a small addition was made to their pay. A *Mont de Piété* was established for the purpose of relieving after their death the widows and orphans, who had previously no other resource but the public charity. The order of Avis, the second of the three orders of knighthood in the kingdom, was particularly devoted to the recompense of military services.

'The twenty-four regiments of infantry had been formed in 1762 into one battalion of ten companies. This battalion was now divided into two, of only five companies each, of which there was one of grenadiers in the first battalion, and one of chasseurs in the second. The complement of the company was one hundred and fifty men, so that the regiment amounted to fifteen hundred, and the total of the infantry to thirty-six thousand men. These troops were but little exercised. The regulations for manœuvres given to them by Count Lippe comprised scarcely any but a few elementary school notions of platoon and battalion. Detachments of men were selected from all the corps, and assembled near the village of Azambuja, in an experimental camp, where they were to

Two more Bradford sketches of Spanish troops; during the winter of 1810–11 La Romana led a contingent of 8,000 Spaniards who served in Portugal, inside the Lines of Torres Vedras. The two infantry grenadiers, of the Regiments de Estramadura and Zaragoza, wear the white uniforms favoured in many Catholic countries; the former has crimson facings and the latter, light green. The 'flames' of the bearskin bonnets are in facing colour and covered with intricate embroidery, shown here as yellow and white. Both figures have brass buttons and fittings and red sabre-knots; the Zaragoza figure has green gaiter trim and tassels. The horseman is probably a soldier of the Villaviciosa Dragoons of 1808; he wears green dolman and breeches, red facings and plume, and yellow buttons. The shako has a white top band and cords, yellow plate, and red cockade. Gauntlets are white, holster covers green edged red, harness brown with white fittings, and sheepskin black

receive an enlarged and uniform instruction, for the purpose of carrying it afterwards into the regiments. This experiment was not productive of the benefit to the army in general that was expected from it.

'The light-infantry could not but appear an excrescence, in a country where the peasants consider it as a sacred obligation to disperse themselves among the rocks, as soon as they hear the firing of the alarm-gun, and to shoot or dispatch with their pikes the armed stranger who violates their territory. However, a corps of light troops, consisting of eight companies of infantry, two squadrons of cavalry, and a battery served by gunners on horseback, was created. It was called the Legion of Alorne, after the Marquis of that name by whom it was commanded.

'The colonies had their military establishment distinct from the European troops. A special corps, *brigada real da marinha*, formed the garrison of the ships.

'We have adverted to the militia. This subsidiary army consisted of forty-eight regiments of one battalion each, distinguished by the name of the districts where they were levied. Men of consequence, selected from among those who reside on their estates, commanded the militia regiments. The State equipped and armed them, and ensured to them local privileges, which were highly valued by the peasants. They clothed themselves at their own cost. They were paid only when on duty, and, with the exception of the annual reviews, they were not called together unless on extraordinary occasions.

'The squadrons of cavalry had each four companies of forty-eight men, a most injudicious plan; for the troops intended to form a unit in the manœuvres ought not to be cut into four for habitual service. Though certain regiments bore the name of dragoons, the cavalry was of a single kind, mounted on horses of unequal size, cuirassed before, armed with muskets, and trained to fight on foot. The Portuguese are graceful and steady horsemen. The complement of the twelve regiments, of four squadrons each, would have amounted to nearly ten thousand horse. There never were more than four thousand five hundred effective, all natives of the country; and it would have been difficult to bring together a greater number, for but few large cattle are bred on the rocks of Portugal, and the Spanish government has at all times taken severe measures to prevent its fine breeds of horses from being drawn out of its territory.

'The four regiments of artillery had their permanent quarters at Fort St Julian, near Lisbon, Viana, in the province in Minho, Elvas, and Faro, in the Algarves. They were composed of ten companies: namely, one of bombardiers, one of sappers, one of miners, and seven of gunners. The sergeants and cadets underwent an examination before they became officers. The service of the *personnel* was not centralized, and each regiment followed its own method. The *materiel* of the fortresses was in confusion, owing to the multiplicity of the calibres. The artillery for battle could not be numerous in a country where nine-tenths of the high roads are impassable for carriages. Not a beast was appropriated to draw the guns, while the court employed two thousand mules for its transports. It was proposed, in case the army should take the field, to have the service of the train of artillery performed by hired men and animals.

'The royal corps of engineers did duty in the kingdom and in the colonies. It was composed of one hundred and forty officers of all ranks. In order to be admitted into this corps, it was necessary to give proof of attainments acquired in attending the complete courses of the higher sciences in the royal academies of fortification and the marine. To the officers of engineers were confided the duty of instruction in the chairs of the military art and mathematics, the construction of maps and reconnoissances, the civil works of bridges and roads, and even the superintendence of the ships belonging to the crown. There were among them a good number of clever men, but nearly strangers to the profession of military engineers. Where should they have learned it? It was a settled point in Portugal for more than a century, that attention should be paid to two fortresses only, Almeida, situated beyond the natural frontier of Portugal, and Elvas, which is not upon any of the roads by which an army can march to Lisbon without crossing the Tagus. The other fortresses, not excepting even those, the erection of which had been imperatively commanded by their position at the principal *debouchés* of the frontier, such as Chaves, Castello-Branco, and Abrantes, were doomed to fall to ruin from age, without its being thought worth while to repair any part of their walls. Some old castles were garrisoned by companies of invalid gunners, called *pese de castello*. The names of all these half-demolished towers and batteries without cannon, were only to be found, in the commissions of some decrepid veterans, who were sent thither with the pompous title of governors.

'No troops in Europe received less pay than the soldiers of Portugal, and yet they were impudently robbed of it, especially in the cavalry, where the companies were paid by the captains. There was not in the establishment either a commissariat of war, or any corps of administrators specially appointed to attend to the welfare of the soldiers. It was the duty of the agents of the treasury, *thesourarias geraes das tropas*, to verify the legality of the payments which they made, and at distant intervals general officers came as inspectors to examine the affairs of the regiments. These were the only two sorts of control to which the colonels and captains were liable.

'As for the general expenses of the army, a junta, which had its agents in the provinces, *junta da direccao geral dos provinsentos das municoes de boca para o exercito*, purchased and distributed among the troops bread and other provisions. Another junta, *junta de real fazenda*, directed the operations of the artillery, and attended to the clothing, equipment, and different appointments. Several essential articles, the muskets among others, came from England. The troops of all arms were clothed in blue. They kept themselves in better condition, and looked better than those of Spain. The army medical service formed part of the duties of the protomedicate, *real junta do protomedicato*. The regimental surgeons were but ignorant manipu-

'The Battle of Busacco, 27 September 1810' – a painting which shows Reynier's men attacking uphill against the Anglo-Portuguese 3rd Division of Sir Thomas Picton. The 88th British and 8th Portuguese Regiments are shown engaging the enemy. Busacco was the battle in which the re-organized Portuguese first showed their quality (*National Army Museum*)

lators, and were not allowed by law to perform medical functions, unless when no civil professor of the healing art happened to be within reach of their garrisons.

'Portugal is the country of assemblies (*juntas*), which never assemble, and of councillors, who never give counsel. It is not on the permanent service only that a greedy idleness erects its scaffolding of places, offices, and salaries; it fastens upon mere plans which the Government approves. The building of a bridge, the draining of a marsh; the embanking of a river, furnish occasion for lavishing the public money on a multitude of persons who never fail to present themselves for the purpose of directing or superintending the works. Thus, in the department of war, it was once proposed to reform the penal code of the army, and to give a new organization to the studs of the kingdom. Immediately there appeared a junta, *ad hoc*, composed of twenty grandees, or persons of consequence, *junta do Codigo penal militare e melhoramento das caudelarias do reino*: but the code was neither reformed, nor the studs improved.

'The Council of War instituted by John IV in 1643, and composed of military chiefs and magistrates, was originally entrusted with the government of the army and the administration of justice in it. To these councillors no other real functions have been left than the trial of general officers and the revision of military proceedings. An auditor, taken from the legal profession, was attached to each regiment stationed at Lisbon. In the garrisons, the prosecution of crimes committed by soldiers was entrusted to the civil judges. Several chapters of the regulations of 1763 are devoted to the formation and the holding of regimental courts-martial. The military penal code, otherwise called Articles of War, *Artigos de Guerra*, was severe; but the national manners proved more powerful than the laws. Justice proceeded with slow step; and notwithstanding the eternal threat of blows with the flat of the sword, shooting, and hanging, the internal discipline sinned rather by indulgence than by severity.

'The Portuguese soldiers would have become excellent had pains been taken to make them so; tolerable officers could also be trained without much difficulty; but the leaders were good for nothing. The State kept about sixty marshals,

Infantry and cavalry of the Portuguese Legion in French service. This finely detailed plate is one of a series commonly known to Continental experts as the *Augsburger Bilder* rather than by its full title of *Charackteristische Darstellung der Vorzüglichsten europäischen Militairs*. The series covers all the major European armies of the period 1802–9. From left to right the figures are as follows – all coats reddish brown, all collars and cuffs red: (1.) Black helmet, yellow fittings, brown lapels and shoulder straps piped red; brown breeches piped white; brown portmanteau and red shabraque both edged white; white sheepskin edged red; black harness, yellow buttons, red turnbacks. (2.) (*Rear*) Red cords, plume and epaulettes; grey rolled coat, brown-hide pack, white piping on coat tails, brown trousers, brass sabre hilt. (3.) White cords, brown lapels piped red, brown turnbacks piped white. (4.) Brass horn on shako; red lapels with white piping and buttons; brown trousers. (5.) (*Seated*) Green shako cords and plume, yellow plate; green epaulettes with yellow crescents; two white or silver stripes on lower sleeve; brown pack and trousers, white buttons. (6.) (*Mounted*) Black astrakhan colpack, silver buttons and epaulettes, red bandolier edged silver, red piping to front of coat, red turnbacks, grey overalls with red side stripe, saddlery as No. 1. (7.) (*Walking*) Brown lapels edged red, silver epaulettes and buttons, red sash and turnbacks, brown breeches, gold sword hilt. (8.) (*Mounted*) Black helmet, yellow chin-scales, coat as No. 1, white waistcoat and breeches, white belts, yellow and black sword scabbard, saddlery as No. 1.

lieutenant-generals, marechals-de-camp, and brigadiers. The Duke de Lafões, as Marshal-general, attached to the person of the sovereign, *marechal-general junto a real pessoa*, headed the list. Several names of Fidalgoes figured among them for form's sake. A lieutenant-general, already advanced in years, Joao Dordaz, had the general inspection of the cavalry; and what little value that arm had was owing to his enlightened measures. The two campaigns in Roussillon and Catalonia brought some talents to light. The chivalrous ardour of the marechal-de-camp, Marquis d'Alorne, the activity and firmness of Gomez Freire de Andrada, the analytical and cool mind of Colonel Don Miguel Pereira Forjaz, were highly extolled. There were but few veterans left of the time of Count Lippe, and these were past active service; but with money and promises that cosmopolitan school might be renewed at pleasure.

'The union of the Ministry of War and of Foreign Affairs in the same person afforded facilities for seeking generals abroad. In 1796 the Government procured the Prince of Waldeck,* who had lost an arm at the siege of Thionville, to take the command of the army. He did not live long, and was succeeded by Count de Goltz, a Prussian, formerly secretary to Frederick II. England also gave several French emigrants to Portugal. In this number were Carlet de la Rosière,

* Waldeck was an amiable man, and went to Portugal to recruit his finances.

who had served with distinction during the seven years' war, under the command of Marshal Saxe and the Count de Broglie, and who was considered as the cleverest staff-officer of the royal army of France; and Count de Viomenil, who had acquired some reputation by finding means to see a little of war, at a time when persons placed on the same line with himself saw nothing of it.† The post of Quarter-master-general of the Army was created for La Rosière. Viomenil received the title of Marshal; but, being thwarted by army and court intrigues, he hastened to quit the kingdom, and never returned to it. Other emigrants of less consequence preceded or accompanied these two general officers. All of them came to Portugal, elated with the idea of becoming a second Schomberg or Lippe. The Portuguese nobility, however, treated them with disdain as mere adventurers. The native officers were jealous of these intruders, because double pay was granted to them.* The soldier, by nature censorious, laughed at chiefs who mutilated his language. Six months were sufficient to extinguish the enthusiasm and to disappoint the schemes of the new-comers. The Portuguese Government derived at this period but little benefit from foreign military men. It neither knew what to do with, or how to do without them.

'An army of forty thousand men, ill-regulated and badly commanded, was but a feeble resource in the difficult crisis in which Portugal had placed herself. . . .

'It is foreign to our purpose to inquire whether it is beneficial to a nation for its sovereign to wear several crowns, or how far the choice of the place where he will fix his court depends on the pleasure of the monarch. The Brazilians and the Portuguese formed one and the same nation, parted in two by the ocean. There was no crime in considering America as a refuge, but only at some distant period, not till after the last battle, and at the last extremity. It would have been a noble spectacle to see the chief of a nation defending the inheritance of his ancestors with the resources of

† But, in consequence of his age and position, he had left off making war, since it began to be carried on upon a large scale.
* Double pay was given to the foreigners, because the pay of this country was absurdly small, and also that it might serve as a substitute for the rewards appropriated exclusively to natives.

talent and the energy of despair, and when the ruins of the country had been driven back to the sea, sailing away amidst the conflagration of Lisbon, to prepare vengeance on another national soil, and to carry back in better days his mutilated household gods to their former home.

'While, however, Don Rodrigo kept an eye on the distant American Portugal, he neglected nothing for the improvement of European Portugal. Lisbon is indebted to him for the institution of a police guard and the lighting of the streets. His opinions and his plans were supported in the council by Don Joao de Almeida, who, after the dismissal of the Duke de Lafões, had, according to custom, united the portfolio of war with that of foreign affairs. Don Joao was not deficient in ability, but he was of a nervous constitution, full of prejudices, and subject to alternate fits of irritation and despondency. The campaign of 1801 had shown how little Portugal could reckon upon her army. A new organization was proposed and adopted by the minister: the plan embraced the recruiting which was to be founded on an exact census of the population, and purged of the abuses which, in Portugal, as in other countries, poison the most salutary institutions; likewise the reform of the militia, the harmonizing of the system of the *ordenances* with the service of the troops of the line, the introduction of the manœuvres practised by that nation which has brought the science of arms to the greatest perfection; in a word, all the branches of the military constitution. A certain number of capable officers were employed to digest the plan for these improvements, which was about to be made public, when the ministry was overthrown. . . .

'The ministers of Portugal conceived that they had saved the vessel of the state, because they had escaped a rock. Since the renewal of hostilities between England and Spain, Lisbon had become the mart for the commerce of the Peninsula, and part of Europe. One hundred and forty thousand bales of cotton annually entered the Tagus, and seventy thousand of them served to supply the manufactories of France. The old warehouses being found insufficient to contain the goods, more extensive ones had been built in the squares and on the quays. The city was enlarging; public prosperity, the outward sign of the wisdom of the national councils, seemed to justify the improvident resignation of the government.

'In this manner did Portugal gently glide into the abyss. The crash of falling Europe scarcely reached the solitary palace of Mafra. Napoleon laid the British islands under interdict. This violent measure destroyed the neutrality of all the states of the Continent. It determined the government of the Prince Regent to equip a fleet in the port of Lisbon; but the army remained dispersed and incomplete. The people did not even know that France refused to admit the envoy of their sovereign to the negociations at Tilsit. The cry of alarm was in vain raised abroad. Dumouriez, the same general who first showed the French Republicans the road to victory, Dumouriez addressed from London to the Portuguese nation a manifesto,* fraught with truth and foresight, to apprize it of the catastrophe with which it was threatened,

---

* During the year 1766 Dumouriez traversed Portugal in every direction. Forty-two years afterwards, at the farthest extremity of Beira-Baixa, we met with two old men who had been his guides, and who told us with what activity of mind the young French officer inquired respecting localities and institutions. The observations made by him during these travels are given in a work entitled *Etat Present du Royaume de Portugal en 1766*, which was printed at Lausanne in 1775. This little volume, amidst a multitude of oversights, and even some important errors, contains valuable pieces of information, which might be regarded as discoveries at the period of their publication.

In 1807 General Dumouriez, forgotten by Europe, was vegetating in London. He conceived the idea of offering his services to the Portuguese, to avert the storm which was ready to burst over them. The moment was favourable. Their two marshals, Goltz and Viomenil, were both absent, and were only bound to the country by the pension which was paid them. Among the other general officers, native or foreign, in the service of Portugal, there was not one who, either from his position or his reputation, had any pretensions to the chief command of an army. Dumouriez was sixty-eight, certainly very old for carrying on war in a mountain country; but his robust constitution gave him confidence, and he still retained a youthful imagination and the greenness of talent.

As a first step, Dumouriez printed a brief narrative of the *Campaigns of Marshal Schomberg in Portugal, from the year 1662 to 1668*, with this motto: *C'est au cœur que je parle et non pas à l'esprit*. The work began and ended with a philippic against France. The old general of the Revolution knew the Portuguese better than they knew themselves. He knew what might be accomplished with a fiery nation, in a country studded with difficulties and strong places, where all the males are soldiers from their birth. He foresaw that a weak prince, surrounded by weak advisers, would hesitate to adopt a courageous resolution; but he hoped that, at the approach of the foreigner, the people would rise against courtiers ready to sacrifice the Portuguese name.

'Portuguese Troops on the March, 1811'. The regimental pioneers can be seen at the head of the column in their aprons, with entrenching tools slung and carbines sloped (*National Army Museum*)

and to make it an offer of his sword. The voice of the warrior was not allowed to echo within the walls of Lisbon. The Court Gazette was the only political compass for the mass of the inhabitants. The ministers conceived that their duties were at an end after they had provided for the flight of the Prince and about a hundred courtiers.

'A nation delivered up, bound hand and foot, to the mercy of its foes, was a sight which could only be exhibited under the pressure of a taciturn despotism, but could never happen in a land of liberty. The publicity of the acts of government, and the easy circulation of written ideas, are the safeguards of national independence. The defensive energy of citizens continually armed, who govern themselves according to constitutional forms, cannot be measured. To the enthusiastic and communicative Portuguese, had they been free, one word would have been sufficient: *There is the enemy!*'

From a British source we have a brief account of the Portuguese forces in W. Bradford's *Sketches of Military Costume in Spain and Portugal, 1814*:

'Portugal established its independence by the victories of Extremos and Villa-viciosa, in the year 1663 and 1664, since which the military force of that kingdom had scarcely been called into action for a century. When Spain declared war against Portugal in 1762, the nominal army consisted of 17,000 men, including 2,400 cavalry, of which, not more than half could be mustered, and these without artillery or engineers. The talents of the German Count de la Lippe who commanded them, and the assistance of the British, enabled this force to resist the Spanish army, who retired at the close of the campaign, after sustaining considerable loss as well from the regulars as the peasants.

'In 1766 the army consisted of 33 battalions, containing 26,000 infantry, and 26 squadrons of cavalry, containing about 4,000 men: the peasantry form a militia of 100,000 men, who serve without pay; engage with fury, and cut off numbers by sudden attacks, and ambuscades.

'The discipline and appearance of these troops is respectable, and they manœuvre well; its organisation is, however, defective in having its battalions divided into 7 companies (one of which are grenadiers) each of 140 men; this formation will not allow of the rapid evolutions of modern tactics, and possesses not a sufficient number of officers. The cavalry is mounted on horses from the provinces of Andalusia, Beira, and Tras os Montes, which are small.

'The artillery composed of 3 battalions was badly disciplined in 1766, and at that period no field pieces were attached to the infantry: the engineers and school attached to it were also in an indifferent state.

'In 1806 the army consisted of 24 regiments of infantry, 12 of cavalry, and 4 of artillery; each regiment of infantry contained (nominally) 1,102 men, that of cavalry 320 men, and 989 formed a

Dighton's painting of a Portuguese Militiaman, 1812; these troops occupied many of the static positions in the Lines of Torres Vedras, freeing the line regiments for service with the field army. The soldier wears an English 'stovepipe' shako with white-over-red tuft and blue and red cockade; the dark blue coat is faced red and has white buttons and shoulder-scales. The trousers are light brown (*Reproduced by gracious permission of Her Majesty the Queen*)

'The armed peasantry form an irregular force of upwards of 100,000 men; since the expulsion of the French, part of the Portuguese force has been formed into legions.

'The staff consists of a marechal general, 3 generals, (1 for each description of force) a quarter master general, about 25 lieutenant generals, 16 major generals, (*Marechaes de Campo*) and about 25 brigadiers.

The pay of a captain is 10,000 Reas. (£2 12s. 0) per month.

That of a soldier is 1,200 Reas. (6s. 3d.) per month.

'The uniform of the general officers and suite is scarlet and gold; that of the infantry dark blue; the cavalry wear light blue, with pantaloons of various colours.

'Almeida covers the province of Beira, and the left bank of the Douro, but it requires a large garrison, and does not cover the capital.

'The right bank of the Tagus is undefended, except by the difficult passes of Idanha, Pena Macor, and Alfayates. Elvas, on the southern side of the Tagus, is strong, but requires a numerous garrison, the forts of La Lippe, and Saint Lucia are on two mountains near it, the first is very strong and requires 2,000 men to defend it, Saint Lucia might be taken with ease.

'The navy which conveyed the Prince Regent to Brazil in 1807, consisted of 8 sail of the line, 4 frigates, and 24 smaller vessels. – Brazil furnishes wood, but naval stores must be derived from other countries. The little kingdom of Algarve produces excellent sailors.'

The following much fuller explanation is taken directly from Oman:

Organisation 1809

'The numbers are from the first complete return available, that of Sept 15 1809 in the Record Office.

INFANTRY OF THE LINE

'N.B. Each regiment consisted of two battalions of seven companies each, which should have numbered 770 officers and men, the regiment totalling 1,550, with staff.

regiment of artillery: the whole force would therefore consist of, infantry 26,448, cavalry 3,840, artillery 3,956, total 34,244. The army is formed into 3 grand divisions, called the divisions of the north, centre, and south; however, in 1801, Portugal could only oppose 15,000 men to the Spaniards.

'Besides the regular troops there are 48 regiments of militia, bearing the names of the principal places in each of the 3 divisions, 16 in each division.

'The police guards, established for the internal security of Lisbon, by de Souza, were taken from among the best troops of the army, and were under the command of the Count de Novion.

'Officers of various European armies, c.1800'. A plate from Friedrich Ludwig von Köller's work *Uniformzeichnung der vorzüglichsten Europäischen Truppen*, published in Kiel in 1802 by C. F. Mohr. Left to right: (1) Officer of Walloon Dragoons – dark blue coat faced pink; silver epaulettes, buttons and hat loop, orange cockade and sash. (2) Royal Prussian Cuirassier Officer, gala uniform – white-over-black plume, white coat faced light blue; silver lace, buttons and aiguilettes; buff waistcoat, silver and black sash and sword knot, gold hilt, buff gloves. (3) Royal Portuguese Infantry Officer – yellow plume, gold hat trim, red within blue cockade (note cruciform shape), silver loop and button; dark blue coat faced lemon yellow, with silver buttons, epaulettes and gorget; crimson sash with silver tassels; silver sword-knot, gold hilt. One copy of this work shows dark blue breeches with silver thigh-knots, another (in Altona) shows white breeches with silver knots. (4) Royal Danish Lieutenant General – white plume, black cockade, gold agraffe and tassels; bright red coat faced light blue, gold lace and buttons, gold epaulettes and belts, gold-hilted sabre with gold and red knot; yellow breeches with gold embroidery, gold trim to boots, silver spurs

Dighton's 'Private, 20th Portuguese Infantry Regiment, 1812'. The Portuguese infantry shako, with its raised front, has given way to the British 'stovepipe' – probably on economic grounds. Britain was exporting large quantities of war material of all kinds to Portugal, and it was only British gold which supported the economy of the country, shattered by occupation and war. Portuguese industry was in no condition to maintain an ever-increasing supply of national patterns. The plate here is brass, the tuft red and white, the cockade blue and red – note that here the cockade is shown as a quartered disc; note also the chin-tapes tied above the crown. The coat is dark blue with yellow facings, scales and buttons; the pack is brown hide (*Reproduced by gracious permission of Her Majesty the Queen*)

	Strength
1st Regt (1st of Lisbon or La Lippe)	1,330
2nd Regt (Lagos or Algarve)	1,301
3rd Regt (1st of Olivenza★)	679
4th Regt (Freire)	1,477
5th Regt (1st of Elvas)	759
6th Regt (1st of Oporto)	1,082
7th Regt (Setubal)	1,312
8th Regt (Evora)	369
9th Regt (Viana)	1,511
10th Regt (2nd of Lisbon)	1,370
11th Regt (1st of Almeida)	1,498
12th Regt (Chaves)	1,491
13th Regt (Peniche)	1,361
14th Regt (Tavira)	1,239
15th Regt (2nd of Olivenza★)	577
16th Regt (Viera Telles)	696
17th Regt (2nd of Elvas)	1,218
18th Regt (2nd of Oporto)	1,371
19th Regt (Cascaes)	1,519
20th Regt (Campomayor)	1,218
21st Regt (Valenza)	193
22nd Regt (Serpa)	1,479
23rd Regt (2nd of Almeida)	1,521
24th Regt (Bragança)	505
Total	27,076

CAZADORES (or CAÇADORES)

N.B. These were single-battalion corps with a proper effective of 770 men (in five companies, four of Cazadores and one of Atiradores – OVP).

	Strength
1st (Castello de Vide)	620
2nd (Moura)	425
3rd (Villa Real)	607
4th (Vizeu)	619
5th (Campomayor)	321
6th (Oporto)	560
Total	3,152

'The 7th, 8th and 9th Cazadores were formed later, out of the three battalions of the Lusitanian Legion. The 10th, 11th and 12th were raised in the year 1811.

'The brigading of the Portuguese regular infantry was practically permanent, very few changes having been made after 1810, when the greater part of the regiments were attached in pairs to the British divisions. The arrangement was as follows, 1811–14:

1st Brigade: 1st (Lisbon) and 16th (Viera Telles) (attached to 1st Division).
2nd Brigade: 2nd (Lagos) and 14th (Tavira).

★ Though named from Olivenza these regiments were actually raised in Northern Beira, with head quarters at Lamego, Olivenza having been ceded to Spain in 1801 at the treaty of Badajoz.

'The Taking of Ciudad Rodrigo, 19 January, 1812' (*National Army Museum*)

3rd Brigade: 3rd (1st of Olivenza) and 15th (2nd of Olivenza) (attached to 5th Division).

4th Brigade: 4th (Freire) and 10th (2nd of Lisbon) (attached to 2nd Division).

5th Brigade: 5th (1st of Elvas) and 17th (2nd of Elvas).

6th Brigade: 6th (Oporto) and 18th (2nd of Oporto).

7th Brigade: 7th (Setubal) and 19th (Cascaes) (attached to 7th Division).

8th Brigade: 8th (Evora) and 12th (Chaves) (attached to 6th Division).

9th Brigade: 9th (Viana) and 21st (Valenza) (attached to 3rd Division).

10th Brigade: 11th (1st of Almeida) and 23rd (2nd of Almeida) (attached to 4th Division).

11th Brigade: 13th (Peniche) and 24th (Bragança).

The 20th (Campomayor) and 22nd (Serpa) were never brigaded.

The 1st and 3rd Cazadores were attached to the Light Division.

The 2nd was attached to the 7th Portuguese Brigade, in the 7th Division.

The 4th was attached to the 1st Portuguese Brigade, in the 1st Division.

The 6th was attached to the 6th Portuguese Brigade.

CAVALRY

'N.B. Each regiment should have had 594 men, in four strong squadrons.

		Strength
1st	(Alcantara Dragoons)	559
2nd	(Moura)	400
3rd	(Olivenca)	394
4th	(Duke of Mecklenburg, Lisbon)	559
5th	(Evora)	581
6th	(Bragança)	578
7th	(Lisbon)	564
8th	(Elvas)	287
9th	(Chaves)	572
10th	(Santarem)	475
11th	(Almeida)	482
12th	(Miranda)	589
	Total	6,040

ARTILLERY

Four regiments with headquarters respectively at (1) Lisbon, (2) Faro in Algarve, (3) Estremos in Alemtejo, (4) Oporto. The total strength was 4,472 officers and men.

'There were also a few garrison companies, largely composed of invalids, which were mainly stationed in the forts round Lisbon. Their force is not given in Beresford's *General State of the Regular Army*.

THE LOYAL LUSITANIAN LEGION

'This abnormal force, under Sir Robert Wilson, comprehended in 1809–10 three battalions of infantry, with an establishment of ten companies and 1,000 men each, one regiment of cavalry of three squadrons, which never seems to have been complete, and one battery of field artillery. Its total force was about 3,500 men. In 1811 the three battalions were taken into the regular army as the 7th, 8th and 9th Caçadores.

ENGINEERS

'There were a few officers of the old army, who were engaged in raising new companies of sappers, which were not yet ready when Beresford's report was drawn up. No figures are there given.

★ ★ ★

'It would appear then that the total Regular force of Portugal in 1809 amounted to about 33,000 foot, 6,300 horse, and 5,000 artillery.

MILITIA

'The Portuguese Militia was raised by conscription, on a local basis, the kingdom being divided into forty-eight regions, each of which was to supply a regiment. These districts were combined into three divisions, called the North, South and Centre, each of which gave sixteen regiments. The unit was a two-battalion corps, with nominally 1,500 men in twelve companies: this number was in practice seldom reached. It was usual to keep the battalions under arms alternately, for periods of two, three, or six months: it was seldom that the whole regiment was embodied at once. In 1809 the whole force was but in process of organization, many corps had not even been officered or armed, and the majority had not commenced to raise their second battalion. The local distribution was as follows:

1st DIVISION, 'THE SOUTH': Comprising Algarve, Alemtejo, and Beira Alta.
Regiments of Lagos, Tavira, Beja, Evora, Villaviciosa, Portalegre, Castello Branco, Idanha, Viseu, Guarda, Trancoso, Arouca, Tondella, Arganil, Covilhao, Lamego.

2nd DIVISION, 'THE CENTRE': Comprising Estremadura and Beira Baixa.
Four Lisbon regiments, and one each from Torres Vedras, Santarem, Thomar, Leyria, Soure, Lousao, Alcazar do Sul, Setubal, Coimbra, Figueira, Aveiro, and Oliveira de Azemis.

3rd DIVISION, 'THE NORTH': Comprising Tras–os–Montes and Entre–Douro–e–Minho.
Regiments of Oporto, Villa de Conde, Braga, Viana, Barcellos, Giumaraens, Penafiel, Arcos, Feira, Barca, Baltar, Mayo, Chaves, Villa Real, Miranda and Braganza.'

'Badajos during the Siege of June 1811' – which Wellington was forced to raise upon the approach of Soult from Andalusia. This painting shows 'the working parties of the 3rd Division, British, and General Hamilton's Portuguese Division. . . .' Hamilton's Division consisted of the 2nd, 4th, 10th and 14th Portuguese Infantry Regiments (*National Army Museum*)

1 Pioneer, 1st or Lippe's Infantry Regiment, 1809–1814
2 Ensign, 21st or Valença Infantry Regiment, 1809
3 Grenadier private, 21st or Valença Infantry Regiment, 1809

MICHAEL ROFFE

Officer, 1st or Alcantara Cavalry Regiment, 1809

1 Lieutenant Colonel of Engineers, 1809
2 Corporal, Atiradore Company, 4th Battalion of Caçadores, 1809
3 Captain, Atiradore Company, 2nd Battalion of Caçadores, 1809

1 Fifer, 1st Battalion of Caçadores, 1810
2 Trooper, 8th or Elvas Regiment of Cavalry, 1809
3 Officer, Loyal Lusitanian Legion, 1808

Officer, Legion of D'Alorna ('Experimental Legion'), 1808

Officer, Chasseurs à cheval, Portuguese Legion, 1809

F

MICHAEL ROFFE

1 Private of Fusiliers, 3rd Infantry Regiment, Portuguese Legion, 1812
2 Officer of Voltigeurs, 1st Infantry Regiment, Portuguese Legion, 1810
3 Officer, Portuguese Legion Infantry, 1809

1 Trumpeter, Chasseurs à cheval of the Portuguese Legion
2 Gunner, Portuguese Artillery, 1809
3 Drummer, Portuguese Legion Infantry

Interesting study of Spanish troops, dated 1812. Wellington's decision to press the assault on Badajos in April of that year was partly based on his distrust of the Spanish garrison he had left in Ciudad Rodrigo, now threatened by Marmont. On the left is a chaplain riding a mule; next, a trooper of the 'Al Garbio' Regiment in dark blue faced yellow, with red and white saddle furniture; and another soldier of this unit is seated, wrapped in his dark blue cloak – note gaiters laced on inside, cut to resemble heavy cavalry boots. Beside him stands a cavalryman in fatigue dress – a yellow cap and sleeved waistcoat, the sleeves of the latter attached with red laces. The grenadier has red facings, and is of the Guadalaxara Regiment (here captioned, *sic*, 'Garda lascara'). On the right is a mixed group of line and militia infantry (*Reproduced by gracious permission of Her Majesty the Queen*)

Uniforms

The Cavalry

Black leather helmet with black combe and peak, black crest and yellow metal fittings, blue within red cockade on the left hand side. Moustaches were worn. Light blue coat with a single row of nine yellow buttons, yellow metal 'wings' on each shoulder. Collar, cuffs, turnbacks and piping in the regimental colours. For parades white breeches and short hussar-style boots with screw-in brass spurs; on campaign, grey buttoned overalls worn over the boots. White bandolier, black pouch, white sabre slings, curved sabre in black and yellow sheath, black sabretasche. Horse furniture light blue with yellow edging, pistol holster covers of black bearskin.

The Artillery

Dark blue coat of infantry style with red collar and cuffs, yellow buttons and turnbacks in the divisional colours as shown.

The Engineers

This all-officer corps wore large cocked hats edged in the button colour, button loop and cockade, white plume with black tip, dark blue coat, yellow buttons and epaulettes.

The Infantry

Black felt and leather shako with raised front, superficially resembling the 1812 pattern British infantry model; brass front band around the bottom of the shako pierced with the regimental number, above this an oval brass plate bearing the Portuguese crest. To the top left-hand side was the blue-within-red cockade* from which (for parades) a white plume issued. Shako cords were mixed blue and the divisional colour with the addition of gold for all ranks above corporal; officers' cords all gold, officers' plumes with a black tip.

Badges of rank:

Lance Corporal –
  one yellow stripe around the cuffs
Corporal –
  two yellow stripes around the cuffs
'Furriel' –
  yellow metal scale 'wings' on both shoulders, the left one with yellow fringes

*The shape is not known for certain – some sources show it as a cruciform arrangement of two pieces of ribbon, others as a 'bow-tie' shape.

Dighton's 'Portuguese Caçadores Regiment No 4', painted in 1812. By this date all the *caçadore* regiments of the Portuguese army are thought to have worn red-brown uniforms faced black, though many soldiers – as here – must have worn the grey British campaign trousers. The shako has an interesting squared peak, similar to the folding peaks of some British caps; the pompon is black, the badge and numeral are white metal, and the cockade is blue and red. The Baker rifle and its black leather equipment were widely used by these light troops (*Reproduced by gracious permission of Her Majesty the Queen*)

Second sergeant and drum major –
 yellow metal scale wings, the right one with a yellow fringe, sabre with yellow knot
Sergeant –
 yellow metal scale wings, both with yellow fringes, sabre with yellow knot

Rank Distinctions (Officers):

All officers wore scale epaulettes (those of the regular army being gold and the militia silver), gold gorgets, red waist sashes, and gold sword knots.

Ensign –
 fringed epaulette on the left shoulder
Lieutenant –
 fringed epaulette on the right shoulder
Captain –
 fringed epaulettes on both shoulders
Major –
 bullion epaulette on left shoulder and fringed epaulette on the right
Lieutenant Colonel –
 bullion epaulette on the right shoulder and fringed epaulette on the left
Colonel –
 two bullion epaulettes
Brigadier General –
 two wrought bullion epaulettes each with one star; plain blue coat with broad gold lace on collars and cuffs

Major General –
 as for brigadier general but collar and cuffs embroidered

Lieutenant General –
 as above but two rows of embroidery on collar and cuffs

Field Marshal –
 as above but all of collar, cuffs and epaulettes are embroidered

Grenadiers wore a grenade badge on their shakos between the lower band and the oval plate, and their dark blue shoulder straps were fringed at the outer ends with mixed blue and divisional colour fringes. Pioneers wore brass crossed-axes on their shakos, grenadier shoulder-strap edging, full beards, and white aprons. Drummers had mixed white and divisional colour lace to collar and cuff edging and across the chest.

The Light Infantry (Caçadores)

Shako as for the line with following differences: the regimental number surrounded by a bugle horn; cords and plume green for *Caçadores*, plume black for *Atiradores*.

Brown coats, yellow buttons, black leatherwork; *Atiradores* had green fringes to the outer ends of their shoulder straps. Across the chest of the jacket ran nine yellow lace stripes (gold for officers). Breeches were white, gaiters black with black leather buttons.

On 11 July 1809 new uniform regulations were published for the light infantry, decreeing that all battalions were to have black facings, distinction being shown only on their buttons. After the battle of Albuera in May 1811 the Loyal Lusitanian Legion (a 'private army' formed by Sir Robert Wilson on 4 August 1808 on instructions from Lord Castlereagh, the British Prime Minister) became the 7th, 8th and 9th *Caçadore* Battalions.

REGIMENTAL COLOUR SEQUENCE
FIRST OR SOUTHERN DIVISION

Infantry	*Collar*	*Cuffs*	*Turn-backs piping and lining*
1st or Lippe's Regiment of Infantry	Blue	White	White
4th or Freire's Regiment of Infantry	Blue	Red	White

The taking of Badajos, 6 April 1812 – one of the bloodiest actions of the whole Peninsular War, in which 1,850 British and 400 Portuguese troops fell. The maddened attackers wreaked their vengeance on the survivors of the Franco-German garrison and on the Spanish citizens without restraint; the orgy of drunken violence is often quoted to the British soldier's discredit by Continental historians, ignoring the fact that this kind of lapse was almost unheard of in Wellington's army but was a commonplace among their own forces (**National Army Museum**)

Two of the categories of German troops which fought with Napoleon's armies in the Peninsular against the Anglo-Portuguese and Spanish forces. *Left* is a Frankfurt voltigeur or rifleman. The Frankfurt battalion was organized on French lines; it served initially with Leval's division, fighting at Talavera, but in 1812 transferred to Darmagnac's division of King Joseph's Army of the Centre. The plate is by Weiland; the plume is black with a yellow tip, the pompon yellow, the cords and plate white, the latter bearing a wheel design. Breeches and jacket are dark green, the collar, cuffs, waistcoat, buttons, and hilt are yellow, and the lapels and thigh embroidery are red. Epaulettes are dark green, the gaiters black with yellow buttons, the sabre strap white. Shako, musket and sabre are all French issue. *Right* is an impression of the Grand Ducal Household Regiment of Würzburg, which fought at Gerona and Barcelona, and suffered so many casualties in these actions and a number of minor engagements that by 1811 it was reduced from two battalions to one. The uniforms illustrated were white with red facings and yellow buttons. The wounded officer has gold epaulettes and gorget, the latter with a silver device; he is supported by a grenadier sergeant with a red plume and pompon, red cords and a gold top band to his shako. The shako plate is brass, bearing an F (for Ferdinand), and is surmounted by a crown. The cockade is red-within dark blue-within yellow. He has red epaulettes, and two yellow rank stripes on a red ground. The fusilier to their right has a light blue company pompon and white cords on his shako; his shoulder straps are white edged red, but otherwise his uniform is the same as the grenadier's

Infantry	Collar	Cuffs	Turn-backs piping and lining
7th or Setubal Regiment of Infantry	Blue	Yellow	White
10th or Lisbon Regiment of Infantry	Blue	Sky blue	White
13th or Peniche Regiment of Infantry	White	White	White
16th or Veira Telles Regiment of Infantry	Red	Red	White
19th or Cascaes Regiment of Infantry	Yellow	Yellow	White
22nd or Serpa Regiment of Infantry	Sky blue	Sky blue	White
Cavalry			
1st or Alcantara Regiment of Cavalry	White	White	White
4th or Meklenburg Regiment of Cavalry	Red	Red	White
7th or Caes Regiment of Cavalry	Yellow	Yellow	White
10th or Santarem Regiment of Cavalry	Blue	Blue	White

'The Battle of Salamanca, 22 July 1812', by R. Simkins – as so often, the British are inaccurately shown wearing the later Belgic shako. Portuguese formations did well at Salamanca: Powers's brigade fought with the 3rd Division, whose head-on attack smashed Thomieres's division, and D'Urban's Portuguese cavalry carried out a damaging charge (*National Army Museum*)

	Collar	Cuffs	Turn-backs piping and lining
Artillery			
1st or Lisbon Regiment of Artillery	Red	Red	White
Light Infantry			
1st or Castillo de Vidé Battalion of Caçadores	Brown	Sky blue	White
4th or Beira Battalion of Caçadores	Sky blue	Sky blue	White

THE SECOND OR CENTRE DIVISION

	Collar	Cuffs	Turn-backs piping and lining
Infantry			
2nd or Lagos Regiment of Infantry	Blue	White	Red
5th or 1st Elvas Regiment of Infantry	Blue	Red	Red
8th or Castello de Vide Regiment of Infantry	Blue	Yellow	Red
11th or Penamacor Regiment of Infantry	Blue	Sky blue	Red
14th or Tavira Regiment of Infantry	White	White	Red
17th or 2nd Elvas Regiment of Infantry	Red	Red	Red
20th or Campo Maior Regiment of Infantry	Yellow	Yellow	Red
23rd or Almeida Regiment of Infantry	Sky blue	Sky blue	Red
Cavalry			
2nd or Moura Regiment of Cavalry	White	White	Red
5th or Evora Regiment of Cavalry	Red	Red	Red
8th or Elvas Regiment of Cavalry	Yellow	Yellow	Red
11th or Almeida Regiment of Cavalry	Blue	Blue	Red
Artillery			
2nd or Algarve Regiment of Artillery	Red	Red	Red
3rd or Estremos Regiment of Artillery	Red	Red	Red

Dighton's 'Officer, 10th Regiment Portuguese Cavalry, dated 1812. The crested helmet of 1808 has been replaced by a bell-topped shako with a red plume, yellow number and chinscales, and blue and red cockade. The coat is dark blue faced and piped red, with gold buttons and epaulettes; the sash is red, the belts buff and the overalls blue strapped with leather (*Reproduced by gracious permission of Her Majesty the Queen*)

	Collar	Cuffs	Turnbacks piping and lining
Light Infantry			
2nd or Moura Battalion of Caçadores	Brown	Red	Red
5th or Campo Maior Battalion of Caçadores	Red	Red	Red

THIRD OR NORTHERN DIVISION

Infantry

3rd or 1st Olivença Regiment of Infantry	Blue	White	Yellow
6th or 1st Oporto Regiment of Infantry	Blue	Red	Yellow
9th or Viana Regiment of Infantry	Blue	Yellow	Yellow
12th or Chaves Regiment of Infantry	Blue	Sky blue	Yellow
15th or 2nd Olivença Regiment of Infantry	White	White	Yellow
18th or 2nd Oporto Regiment of Infantry	Red	Red	Yellow
21st or Valença Regiment of Infantry	Yellow	Yellow	Yellow
24th or Bragança Regiment of Infantry	Sky blue	Sky blue	Yellow

Cavalry

3rd or Olivença Regiment of Cavalry	White	White	Yellow
6th or Bragança Regiment of Cavalry	Red	Red	Yellow
9th or Chaves Regiment of Cavalry	Yellow	Yellow	Yellow
12th or Miranda Regiment of Cavalry	Blue	Blue	Yellow

Artillery

4th Oporto Regiment of Artillery	Red	Red	Yellow

Light Infantry

3rd or Tras os Montes Battalion of Caçadores	Brown	Yellow	Yellow
6th or Oporto Battalion of Caçadores	Yellow	Yellow	Yellow

ORGANISATION

Under Count Lippe, each infantry regiment had seven companies: the First, or Colonel's Company of 116 men; the Second, or Lieutenant Colonel's Company, the Third, or Major's, company and four Captains' Companies all of 114 men. The regimental staff consisted of an adjutant, a quartermaster, a chaplain, auditor, surgeon and six assistant surgeons, drum-major, armourer and provost, giving 814 men in all. In addition, any number of '*aggregadoes*' on half pay and junior to regular equivalent ranks could be attached.

Cavalry

N.B. (1809) Due to horse shortage, the following regiments were in fact dismounted: 2nd, 3rd, 6th, 9th and 12th.

Count Lippe formed his cavalry regiments on a low scale; each troop comprised 3 officers, 5

N.C.Os, 1 trumpeter, 1 farrier and 30 men. There were eight troops to each regiment (320 men). Beresford changed this to conform to English establishment of 520 men.

Artillery

Four regiments each of 3- or 6-pdr. guns prior to 1809, but Beresford introduced the light 9-pdr.; 12 guns to a battery.

Artillery and Engineers were controlled by the equivalent of our M.G.O. (Master General of Ordnance).

MILITIA REGIMENTS – 1809
First Division

Lagos Regiment of Militia	Viseu
Tavira	Guarda
Beja	Trancoso
Evora	Arouca
Villaviciosa	Tondella
Portalegre	Arganil
Castello Branco	Covilhao
Idanha	Lamego

Second Division

4 Lisbon Regiments	
Torres Vedras	Alcacer do Sal
Santarem	Setubal
Thomar	Coimbra
Leiria	Figueira
Soure	Aveiro
Lousao	Oliveira de Azemis

Third Division

Oporto	Baltar
Villa de Conde	Feira
Braga	Barca
Viana	Mayo
Barcellos	Chaves
Guimarães	Villa Real
Penafiel	Miranda
Arcos	Bragança

Loyal Lusitanian Legion

In 1808 the Loyal Lusitanian Legion was formed in Oporto. It consisted of two infantry battalions or divisions of 1,000 men each (the second division was crushed in infancy by Soult, but later reformed); one regiment of cavalry, and one battery of artillery (four 6-pounder guns; two howitzers). Uniforms were in the British style, as were drill and discipline.

Infantry uniform – green with green facings
Cavalry uniform – green with white facings
Artillery uniform – green with black facings

Stragglers from Sir John Moore's army swelled its ranks, and it had an excellent fighting record. After Albuera the Legion was converted into the 7th, 8th and 9th Caçadore battalions and lost its original uniform.

THE PORTUGUESE LEGION

When Napoleon conquered Portugal in 1807 he dismissed half the Portuguese army. Some 6,000 to 8,000 men were retained and formed an army corps whose generals and general staff were Portuguese. They were sent to Salamanca, Bayonne and finally to Grenoble where a *Portuguese Legion* was formed by decree of 18 May 1808. It was to consist of six light infantry regiments (although only five were ever formed), two regiments of *Chasseurs à cheval*, and a battery of artillery (whose life was very short). The commander of the Legion was Don Pedro de Almeida, Marquis of Alorna; the Divisional General was Gomez Freyre, the Brigadier Generals de Pamplona and Carcome, and the Chief of Staff Souza.

Colonels of regiments were as follows:
1st Regiment –
   Joachim Albuquerque von Saldanha
2nd Regiment –
   D. Thomas, Marquis von Ponte Lima
3rd Regiment –
   Freyre Pego, then Castro
4th Regiment –
   Botelho Alvaro, Graf von San Miguel
5th Regiment –
   Vasconçellos
1st Cavalry Regiment –
   de Aguiar
2nd Cavalry Regiment –
   Marquis von Tole

This Legion was increased in 1809 by a Demi-Brigade of grenadier and voltigeur companies taken from various Portuguese battalions. By 2 May 1811, however, it was reduced to three infantry regiments, and in November 1813 it was disbanded completely. On 5 May 1814 all those Portuguese still in French service were disarmed and handed over to their own government.

Uniform: Spencer (with half lapels) of Francis-

Interesting study of Portuguese and Spanish troops dated 1812. The 3rd Caçadores on the left wear brown faced red, as worn in the earlier period by the 2nd and 5th Battalions – the 3rd should have yellow facings. Officers wear crimson sashes and gold epaulettes, and the drummer has red epaulettes and brown breeches piped white. The brass drum has red hoops. The Spanish cavalry (Villaviciosa light dragoons) wear green with red facings, white lace and buttons, red plumes, and red shabraques trimmed white (*Reproduced by gracious permission of Her Majesty the Queen*)

can brown colour; lapels, collar, cuffs and turnbacks red; white piping. Brown trousers with a double red stripe. The shako was the Portuguese *barretina* pattern with raised front 6 cm higher than the rest of the hat, and brass front plate and chinscales. Grenadiers had red epaulettes, plumes and cords and had grenades on their turnbacks in white. Voltigeurs had yellow-over-red plumes, green cords and green lapels with white hunting horns on the turnbacks. The centre companies had brown 'duck's-foot' shoulder straps piped red and a red pompon on the shako. White buttons. The pouches of grenadiers and voltigeurs bore white grenades or hunting horns.

The *Chasseurs à cheval* had the same coat as the infantry, with red lapels, and wore the same trousers over half-boots. Headgear was a black lacquered helmet with black peak, brass combe and chin-scales, black crest of wool and a brown turban edged in brass with a round plate in the front centre. Portmanteau round, red edged in white; grey mantle; white sheepskin with red vandyked edging. Other equipment as for French *Chasseurs à cheval*.

A battalion of Portuguese *Pioniers* was raised in 1812 and existed until 1814. It was organized, equipped and dressed completely on French lines.

In 1809 the entire Portuguese Legion was mobilized as a brigade in the 3rd Division of Oudinot's Second Corps in the war against Austria. The order of battle of the 3rd Division is reproduced below:

Divisional Commander – General Grandjean
1st Brigade (General Marion)
10eme Regiment d' Infanterie Légère – 3 battalions
     (Colonel Berthezène)
2nd Brigade (General Lorencez)
3eme Regiment de la Ligne – 3 battalions
     (Colonel Schobert)
57eme Regiment de la Ligne – 3 battalions
     (Colonel Charrière)
3rd Brigade (General Brun)
72eme Regiment de la Ligne – 3 battalions
105eme Regiment de la Ligne – 3 battalions
     (Colonel Blanmont)
Total of French infantry –   155 officers
                              5,928 N.C.Os and men
4th (Portuguese) Brigade (General Carcome-Lego)
13th demi-brigade Portugaise – 3 battalions
Chasseurs à cheval Portugaise – 2 squadrons
Total of Portuguese troops –   65 officers
                              1,539 N.C.Os and men
                                140 horses

Divisional Artillery and Engineer Park (Colonel Villeneuve)
  34 officers
  1,827 N.C.Os and men
  1,983 horses

Two of the Portuguese infantry battalions distinguished themselves under Oudinot at the battle of Wagram (5–6 July 1809) but had arrived too late to take part in the preceding battle of Aspern–Essling on 21–22 May 1809 (in which Napoleon experienced his first defeat in the field).

The Portuguese Legion took part in the 1812 campaign but not as a composite formation; it was split up between the II Corps (Marshal Oudinot) and the III Corps (Marshal Ney) as shown below:

II CORPS (Marshal Oudinot, Duke of Reggio)

6th Infantry Division (General Legrand)
  26th French Light Infantry Regiment – 4 battalions
  19th French Line Infantry Regiment – 4 battalions
  56th French Line Infantry Regiment – 4 battalions
  128th* French Line Infantry Regiment – 2 battalions
  3rd Portuguese Infantry Regiment – 2 battalions

(Actually this unit* was recruited from Bremen, an old Hanseatic town which had been incorporated into France in 1810)

Two fascinating Dighton paintings of Spanish volunteer and irregular officers in 1813. The relative freedom to manoeuvre enjoyed by Wellington's Anglo-Portuguese field army was entirely due to the tremendous strain placed upon the French armies of occupation by the Spanish popular forces; internal communications and supply distribution suffered appallingly, and the morale of the French conscripts was not improved by the medieval savagery with which the Spaniards treated prisoners unlucky or foolish enough to be taken alive. *Left* **is 'Jose de Espin, one of Don Juan Martin's chiefs'. The black hat bears a yellow and red cockade with the FVII cypher of the exiled Spanish king Fernando; the rest of the costume is green with silver trim and buttons. Note the death's-head badges on the collar and the hat-band.** *Right* **is an 'Officer of the Loyal distinguished Cadiz Volunteers'. He wears a red cockade, white plume and white metal plate on his black hat. The red-brown jacket has orange facings and white lace and buttons; silver epaulettes are worn, and note the odd silver badge on the forearm. The waistcoat is white, the breeches yellow, the sash crimson, the sword hilt and knot gold, and the boot trim and tassels silver. These semi-regular volunteer units made up the bulk of the Spanish armies by a late stage of the war, and often suffered appallingly when brought into the field against the far more professional, better trained, better equipped and infinitely better led French (*Reproduced by gracious permission of Her Majesty the Queen*)**

III CORPS (Marshal Ney, Duke of Elchingen)

10th Infantry Division (General Ledru)
  24th French Light Infantry Regiment – 4 battalions
  26th French Line Infantry Regiment ⎫ 3 or 4
  29th French Line Infantry Regiment ⎬ battalions
  72nd French Line Infantry Regiment ⎭ each
  1st Portuguese Infantry Regiment – 2 battalions
11th Infantry Division (General Razout)
  2nd Illyrian Regiment*

*Originally an Austrian Border Infantry Regiment which was transferred to French service in 1809.

The battle of Vittoria, 21 June 1813. This painting captures something of the spirit of this decisive Allied victory, when the French were forced to flee over rough ground and lost their entire artillery and baggage train. Since King Joseph's treasury and the riches of many refugee Spanish grandees were also with the army, the British soldier enjoyed a day and a night of looting such as he had seldom dreamed of and never experienced. The battle marked the final ruin of the French cause in the Peninsula, and was celebrated throughout free Europe. The Tsar of Russia ordered the singing of a special *Te Deum* throughout his realm (**National Army Museum**)

4th French Line Infantry Regiment	4 or 5 battalions each
12th French Line Infantry Regiment	
93rd French Line Infantry Regiment	
2nd Portuguese Infantry Regiment	– 2 battalions

The *Chasseurs à cheval* of the Portuguese Legion was also involved in the Russian campaign and fought at Borodino, as did their infantry comrades. Although not finally disbanded until 1813, very few members of the Legion survived the bitter Russian winter and 'Regiments' consisted of handfuls of disease-ridden, ragged, frostbitten tramps.

The Plates

A1 Pioneer, 1st or Lippe's Infantry Regiment, 1809–1814

Due to the fact that the pioneers of each battalion were frequently working ahead of their comrades, making roads and bridges in rough country and with the minimum of comforts, they were usually permitted to grow full beards. Even today, the pioneer sergeant of each British infantry battalion can be seen sporting his 'full set'. Instead of the normal infantry musket, the pioneers carried carbines slung over their shoulders thus leaving their hands free to use their large axes.

A2 Ensign, 21st or Valença Infantry Regiment, 1809

The similarity between this *barretina* shako and the British 'Belgic' model of 1812–13 (which it is supposed to have inspired) is clear to see. In his *Sketches of Military Costume in Spain and Portugal* Bradford shows the fringes of officers' sashes as silver. The late René North, in set no. 24 of his interesting *Paint-Your-Own* Cards, shows two officers both with red tassels. Bradford also shows the divisional coloured edging of the coat to have been a wide stripe down the front, wider than the button diameter – another item of detail omitted by North. The colour of the 21st Infantry is copied from a watercolour in the Lisbon *Museu Militar*. The cyphers in each corner are crowned 'FPR' – for the Prince Regent of Portugal – and the motto in gold reads clockwise from the 'six o'clock' position JULGAREIS QUALHE MAS EXCELENTE SE (this last word immediately above the crown) SERDO MUNDO REI DE TAL GENTE. The title on the lower label reads REGIMENT°.N°XXI.

A3 Grenadier private, 21st or Valença Infantry Regiment, 1809

The grenadiers' fringed wings are an imitation of the distinctions worn by their comrades in the grenadier companies of the British infantry. The details of the back of the coat would also seem to be modelled after the British pattern.

By 1813 the Spanish army was undergoing a measure of reform, and some formations at least – notably Morillo's division, which fought well at Vittoria and in the Pyrenees – were approaching a standard which enabled Wellington to use them in his field army. These two Dighton paintings illustrate Spanish cavalry of the period. *Left* is 'An Officer of Fernando VII Hussars'; the busby is black with red bag and plume and silver scales and cords. The dolman and pelisse are green with silver lace and buttons, the latter with black fur trim; the facings of the dolman, and the breeches, are buff. The sabretasche and harness are black, the saddlecover is white sheepskin, the shabraque is green trimmed with silver, and the stallion is unbelievable! *Right* are two troopers of the 'Catalan Lancer Corps of Baron d'Erolles'. The helmet has a brown fur crest, green plume, and black, yellow and red cockade. Jacket and breeches are green, with white buttons and black side-stripe (*Reproduced by gracious permission of Her Majesty the Queen*)

B Officer, 1st or Alcantara Cavalry Regiment, 1809

Here, as in the case of Plate A3, the source is Bradford's *Sketches*. Once again, the divisional piping (1st Division, thus white) is very broad down the coat front. The shoulder scales are very British. Finding sufficient cavalry mounts in the Peninsula was a great problem for all the armies engaged in the long and bitter struggle there, and the quality of the Portuguese cavalry – even if very much higher than that of the Spanish – was not really equal to that of the British or French armies or to that of the various German states.

The battle of the Pyrenees, 28 July 1813. A study of some extraordinarily unconvincing uniforms, both British and French! Soult's attempted reinvasion of northern Spain gave Wellington some bad moments, but never had any long-term chance of success (*National Army Museum*)

C1 Lieutenant Colonel of Engineers, *1809*

From the monumental hat and the eagle-headed sabre hilt, it is clear that the Corps of Portuguese Engineers was something of an élite body, even if only in sartorial matters. In those days it was common for engineers to be a small corps composed mainly of officers who had studied mathematics, engineering and fortifications. The labour force, required to put their plans into action in the field, was often provided by the infantry not actively engaged in fighting, and the men who worked were quite well paid in addition to their military pay. (It must be said here that soldiers on campaign in Napoleonic times frequently went for months without pay and thus this extra source of income was quite popular – although the tasks were often dangerous, as in the case of constructing siege parallels under the guns of a hostile fortress.)

C2 Corporal, Atiradore Company, 4th Battalion of Caçadores, *1809*

The best shots in each battalion would have been concentrated in the *Atiradore* or 'Sharpshooters' Company and probably equipped with rifles (almost certainly the famous British Baker model). The rest of the battalion would generally have used the smoothbore musket, as it was considered in those days that too high a proportion of rifles to muskets was disadvantageous. This prejudice was based on the mechanical defects of the rifle, then in its infancy. Although much more accurate than the musket, the rifle was more difficult to load and the rifling quickly became fouled after a few shots, making it almost impossible to keep up fire for a long period. The black leatherwork and the brown clothing represented the first attempts of the Portuguese to delve into the mysteries of camouflage. The light infantry were taught the hunter's skills of fieldcraft, and also took advantage of cover when fighting in extended order.

C3 Captain, Atiradore Company, 2nd Battalion of Caçadores, *1809*

Here again, the British influence in the uniform of the Portuguese army can be seen; the chest lace, red waist sash and the light cavalry style sabre carried by officers of rifle battalions are all very similar to contemporary British items. Wellington's light troops played a vital part in his method of defeating the supposedly invincible French columns of assault. By out-gunning the voltigeur screen (which really was the key to victory for the columns) the British and Portuguese light troops made sure that their own main body, drawn up in the old-fashioned, two-deep line behind them, were still in excellent shape and full of fight when the ponderous French columns approached. The light troops withdrew when the two main bodies neared one another, and the inevitable outcome of the line versus column contest in the Peninsular War was that the column was shot to pieces by the line and was sent reeling back in defeat.

D1   Fifer, 1st Battalion of Caçadores, 1810
As marks of his status, the fifer (or bugler, as was his main battlefield function) had his own uni-

Dighton paintings of two Spanish field officers of the last period of the Peninsular War, valuable for the details of contemporary clothing styles. *Left* **is the Falstaffian figure of Don Juan de Gonzales, colonel of the Spanish Infantry Regiment of Toledo. He wears a reddish-brown uniform faced yellow with silver lace and buttons. There are three silver stripes of rank on the sleeve – one on the cuff and two above it. The point should be made that in view of the chaotic logistic situation with which both sides had to contend in the Peninsular War, the brown local cloth was used in enormous quantities by all nationalities.** *Right,* **in a red coat of distinctly British appearance, is a field officer of the Regiment of the Cortes; he has white facings and gold lace and buttons, a crimson sash, white breeches, black belt, gold sword furniture and knot, and black boot tassels. For some reason the gold loop and button on his hat secure a red and blue cockade instead of the usual Spanish red or red and yellow. His plume is red (***Reproduced by gracious permission of Her Majesty the Queen***)**

form distinctions in the form of special lace decoration to collar, cuffs and chest of his jacket. This figure is shown in the later uniform, when all Caçadore battalions wore black facings.

37

D2 Trooper, 8th or Elvas Regiment of Cavalry, 1809
The system of coloured facings used in the Portuguese army at this period was introduced by the Graf von der Lippe who probably copied the Prussian method of indicating the seniority of regiments within brigades by a standardized use of colour coding. This system was:

    1st Regiment – white
    2nd Regiment – red
    3rd Regiment – yellow
    4th Regiment – blue

The same system is used in the West German *Bundeswehr* today to indicate seniority of brigades within a division, and the colours are shown on the edging to the divisional arm badge. The Elvas cavalry regiment, being in the second division, had red piping and lining to its coat, and as third senior cavalry regiment in that division, yellow collar and cuffs.

D3 Officer, Loyal Lusitanian Legion, 1808
The figure is shown here in the British 'rifle' uniform which was so popular with many of the legions and foreign corps raised for British service during this period. Officer status is indicated by the red silk waist sash and the light cavalry sabre. The Legion was practically destroyed at Albuera; the cavalry and artillery were disbanded, the men going to join their infantry comrades as the new 7th, 8th and 9th Caçadore battalions in 1811.

E Officer, Legion of D'Alorna ('Experimental Legion'), 1808
The Experimental Legion was the only serious attempt made by the Portuguese to modernize their army prior to 1808, and even this formation was only half-heartedly pursued. The infantry of this Legion wore slightly tapered cylindrical shakos (probably of the English light infantry type). The character of the uniform worn here is that of light troops and the horse furniture and harness reinforce this impression.

F Officer, Chasseurs à cheval, Portuguese Legion, 1809
There are several sources of pictorial information on the Portuguese Legion, but this multiplicity tends to increase the confusion which surrounds the details of the dress of this corps rather than to decrease it. In order of apparent reliability the major sources are:

1. Faber du Four – a Württemberg artillery officer who made sketches from life (or death) during the 1812 campaign.

2. The *Augsburger Bilder* – a series of engravings which appeared in the early nineteenth century.

3. Lienhart und Humbert, *Les Uniformes Francais...*, Volume V.

4. The collection of paper cut-out soldiers in the Strassburg museum.

This latter source was used by the late René North for his series of six cards on the infantry of the Legion, but I must confess that my observations of the same little figures differ from his in several respects, e.g. the design of the cap plate and the amount of silver embroidery on the officers' coats. The officer shown here is taken from the *Augsburger Bilder*, and the same illustration appears in Ribeiro's work, *La Légion Portugaise*; it is in the Dubois de l'Etang collection in the Musée de l'Armée.

G1 Private of Fusiliers, 3rd Infantry Regiment, Portuguese Legion, 1812
This figure is based on the folio of engravings made in Russia by Faber du Four. Although the man wears a bugle badge on his shako, his shoulder straps indicate that he is a fusilier. It is quite likely that he has picked up the shako of a fallen comrade of the Voltigeur Company to replace his own which was lost or damaged.

The Portuguese Legion in French service, 1809–13: a plate (no. 130) from Marbot's *Costumes Militaires Français*, Paris, 1860. Unfortunately, uniform detail in these plates is known to have taken second place to artistic composition in some cases. All these figures wear reddish-brown coats with red facings, white buttons, and white piping. (*Left to right*): (1) Chasseur à cheval – black helmet with black crest, brown fur turban; yellow front badge, crown strut and chin-scales, red plume. White belts and bandoliers, steel scabbard, brass hilt, white strap and knot. White sheepskin edged red, brown portmanteau edged red, black harness with brass fittings. (2) Private of Voltigeurs – green shako cords, yellow over red plume, green epaulettes with yellow crescents, yellow shako plate. (3) Officer of Voltigeurs – yellow over red plume, white cockade, gold loop and button; red sash, gold epaulettes and gorget; gold sword-hilt and knot. (4) Grenadier – yellow shako plate; red cords, plume and epaulettes; French M1777 musket.

01702 473986

```
 1865
  350
 ----
 2215
 1.360
 ------
 1865
```

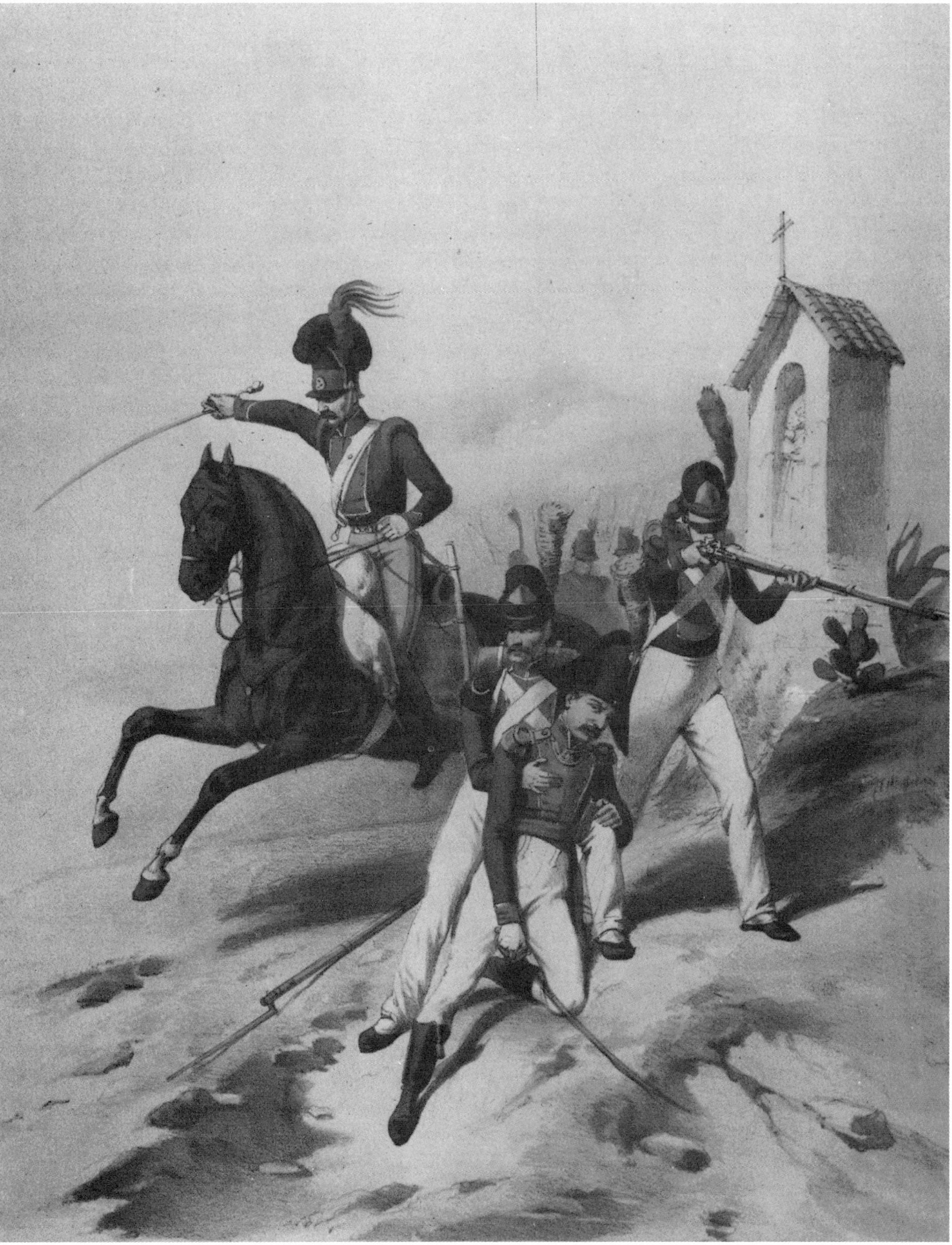

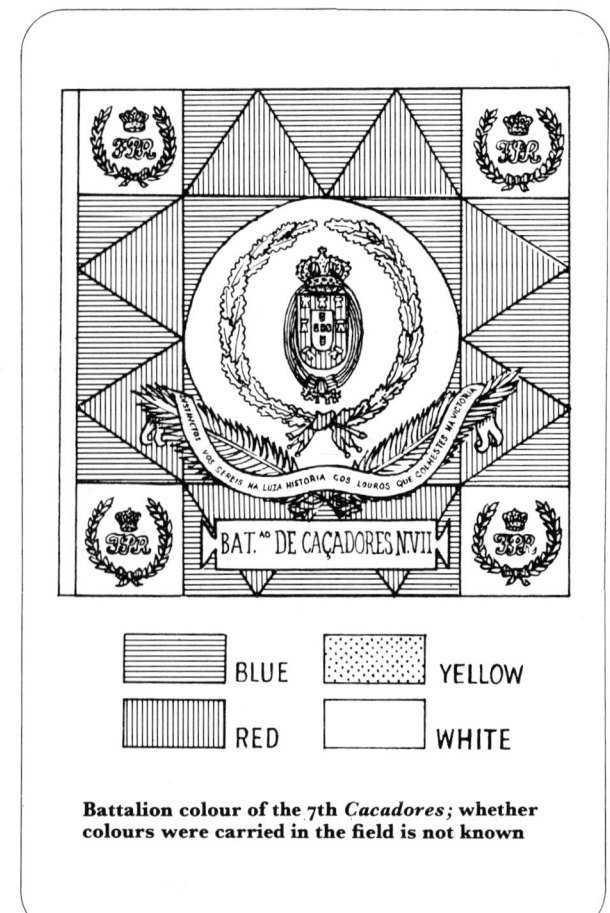

Battalion colour of the 7th *Cacadores*; whether colours were carried in the field is not known

G2 Officer of Voltigeurs, 1st Infantry Regiment, Portuguese Legion, 1810

The yellow-over-red plume is peculiar for a French-satellite unit; French voltigeurs usually had yellow over green plumes. The red waist sash is also an oddity which the French obviously allowed the Portuguese Legion to retain; the *Augsburger Bilder* also show an officer with a red waist sash.

G3 Officer, Portuguese Legion Infantry, 1809

This view is taken from the little paper figures in Strasburg museum. The decoration is so gaudy that the figure could easily be mistaken for a drum major!

H1 Trumpeter, Chasseurs à cheval of the Portuguese Legion

This figure – based on a plate in the Boeswiliwald Collection – is dressed in the conventional reversed colours worn by most drummers and trumpeters of this period. The Carl Collection shows a trumpeter dressed entirely as for the soldiers except that his helmet crest is red and he has silver edging to his collar, cuffs and lapels.

H2 Gunner, Portuguese Artillery, 1809

This man belongs to the foot artillery and thus wears infantry-type equipment as the gun crews marched behind the guns. In the horse artillery the crews rode either on the team horses, the cannon limber (in the Austrian army also on the gun trails) or on extra horses (these were usually reserved for N.C.Os and officers).

H3 Drummer, Portuguese Legion Infantry

This figure is based on the Strassburg museum paper cut-out collection; he is portrayed without shako cords, sabre or drum apron but these have not been added (this is in order that the reader may form his own opinion of the reliability of these figures). The cap plate shows an oval, horizontally divided into three parts, under a five-pointed crown and over a cross. The oval is surrounded by what appear to be arabesques but they could equally well have been flags, cannons etc.